SUPERHEROES

Edited by Caroline Clayton and Jason Page

Written by Claire Watts
and Robert Nicholson

WORLD BOOK / TWO-CAN

SUPERHEROES

This edition published in
the United States in 1997
by World Book Inc.
525 W. Monroe
Chicago, IL 60661
in association with
Two-Can Publishing Ltd.

**For information on other World Book products,
call 1-800-255-1750, x 2238.**

ISBN: 0-7166-4503-3

Printed in Hong Kong

1 2 3 4 5 6 7 8 9 10 99 98 97 96

Design by Elizabeth Bell. Art directed by Catherine Page. Picture research by Debbie Dorman and Sam Riley. Production by Lis Clegg. Additional research by Amanda Tomlin. With thanks to Richard Holliss and Mick Norman.

CONTENTS

SUPER POWERS

Some have special powers, others have only their quick wits

to rely on – but they all have what it takes to be a hero!

Picture the scene: the world is threatened by terrible danger at the hands of some dastardly villain. Time is running out. Is there anyone who can save the day? We need someone strong, someone fearless – we need a hero!

This isn't just the plot of an action-packed film, it's a story that's been told again and again – ever since people first began to entertain each other with amazing stories.

Often they started as tales about real people but, as the stories were passed from one person to another, they became more and more exaggerated. A fight against three people became a battle against 10 and then 100 fearsome enemies. A favorite weapon became an invincible magic tool.

Most legendary heroes have some kind of superhuman powers. The heroes of ancient Greek legends are usually related to the gods. This means they are extra strong, extra clever, and always have luck on their side. The best known of them, Hercules, was only a baby when he strangled two snakes sent to kill him!

MAGIC POWERS

Some heroes are also helped by magic. Odin, the Vikings' most important god, had an invincible spear called *Gungnir*. He also had two ravens which perched on his shoulders and flew off to spy on his enemies. Odin's son, Thor, had a hammer called *Mjolnir* ("the destroyer"), ▶

HERCULES

Hercules is famous for the 12 tasks, or "labors," set for him by King Eurystheus of Tiryns. These included killing monsters, cleaning a stable by diverting a river, and taming a herd of man-eating horses. He proved his amazing strength many times, once even holding up the sky in place of the giant Atlas.

SCHEHERAZADE

The husband of this Persian heroine used to kill each of his wives the morning after he married her. But clever Scheherazade told him a story every night, always stopping at such an exciting point that he would let her live to finish it. After a thousand and one nights, the king found he was too much in love with Scheherazade to kill her.

SPECIAL SKILLS

ODIN

Odin was the Norse god of war. He so loved education and poetry that he gave up his right eye to drink from the well of knowledge.

THOR
The Norse god of thunder, Thor, got into frequent fights with giants. One of them was Skrymir, a frost giant so big that Thor slept in the thumb of his empty glove thinking he was inside a house!

which returned like a boomerang whenever he threw it. He also had a magic belt that doubled his strength.

But not all heroes have superhuman skills or magic powers. Some have only their own wits to rely on. Odysseus, for example, captured the city of Troy by hiding his Greek army inside a huge wooden horse. The Trojans thought it was a gift from the Greeks – but they got an unpleasant surprise when Odysseus' men jumped out!

FATAL FLAW
Few heroes are totally invincible, though. Most have one weakness that can destroy them.

With Superman it's the mineral kryptonite. In the case of Achilles, the great Greek warrior of the Trojan War, it was his heel. When he was a baby, his mother dipped him in the magic River Styx which made his whole body invulnerable – except the heel by which he was held. He was finally killed when a poisoned arrow struck him on it. That's why someone's weak point is often known as his "Achilles heel."

Turn page for more heroic happenings!

TASTE FOR ADVENTURE

When they're not saving the world, heroes are usually on quests. These are long, dangerous journeys to search for a special place or object. King Arthur's knights, for example, went on a quest to find the Holy Grail (see pages 8-9).

In the cause of a quest, a hero might face all manner of perils and challenges to test strength, courage, and honor to the very limits. But for a hero that's all in a day's work!

AENEAS

Aeneas was a Trojan warrior who escaped the destruction of Troy carrying his father on his back. His adventures took him to Crete, Thrace, North Africa, Sicily, and the underworld. Eventually he made his way northward to Latium, where he became one of the founders of the city of Rome.

BOADICEA

Legends soon grow up about real people who act in extraordinary or brave ways. In A.D. 60 Boadicea (or Boudicca), the queen of a British tribe called the Iceni, led a rebellion against Roman invaders. Her army defeated the Roman troops three times before being overcome in A.D. 61, after which she committed suicide. It didn't take long before legendary tales of the astonishing "killer queen" were being passed on.

GIANT KILLER!

The tale of the brave young shepherd who sent a giant to his grave

LONG AGO, THE PHILISTINES WERE FIGHTING THE PEOPLE OF ISRAEL...

WHAT ARE WE GOING TO DO? NO ONE WILL EVER BEAT THE PHILISTINE CHAMPION!

EVERY DAY, THE PHILISTINES SENT OUT THEIR CHAMPION, GOLIATH.

CHOOSE A MAN TO COME OUT AND FIGHT ME. IF HE WINS, WE WILL BECOME YOUR SERVANTS!

UNBELIEVABLE! HE MUST BE OVER NINE FEET TALL!

AT LAST, SOMEONE STEPPED FORWARD TO FIGHT FOR ISRAEL...

I WILL GO AND FIGHT GOLIATH.

BUT, DAVID. YOU'RE ONLY A BOY – AND HE'S A GIANT.

I'VE KILLED LIONS AND BEARS. I'M NOT SCARED OF GOLIATH!

THESE FIVE STONES – **AND MY FAITH** – WILL BE A MIGHTIER WEAPON THAN THE PHILISTINE'S SWORD!

SO DAVID SET OFF CARRYING NOTHING BUT HIS SLINGSHOT AND FIVE STONES...

IS THIS A JOKE? COME HERE, BOY, AND I WILL TEAR YOU TO PIECES.

BUT DAVID SLUNG A STONE AT GOLIATH...

...AND HIT HIM SQUARELY ON THE FOREHEAD, KILLING HIM...

HOORAY!

DAVID – OUR HERO!

Not all heroes come out on top just because they are bigger, stronger, or have special powers. Some win the day in spite of their small size.

According to the Bible, the Israelites had been at war with the Philistines for many years. But armed with just a slingshot and five stones, David managed to kill their prize fighter, the giant Goliath. Then he cut off Goliath's head and presented it to the king.

David became king of Israel and reigned from about 1000 to 965 B.C. He defeated the Philistines and united the tribes of Israel. He also made Jerusalem the spiritual center of Israel by moving the Ark of the Covenant to the city. The Ark was a sacred chest that contained the Ten Commandments. It was this treasure that became the star attraction in the first Indiana Jones movie (see pages 18-19).

STATUESQUE

★ Many famous sculptors, including Michelangelo and Donatello – and we're not talking turtles here – have turned their hand to carving the legendary boy David in stone. Donatello's first David (1408) showed the hero with Goliath's head at his feet. But his more famous bronze statue, shown here, became one of the most important sculptures in the world. This graceful work of art portrays the classical idea of beauty – the human body.

Legend has it that Arthur had no idea he was to be King when he was growing up.

There are many strange tales surrounding King Arthur of Camelot. Legend has it that his brother Kay, struggling on the tournament field, cried out for a sword. Arthur spotted one standing upright with its blade buried deep in a great stone. Little did he know that by removing the sword from the stone he would become the king of Britain.

KNIGHT LIFE
In the Middle Ages many lords in Europe had knights. These were warriors trained to fight on horseback. At first any man could become a knight, but buying armor and keeping a horse became an expensive business. Eventually only wealthy men could afford it.

This one will do! No one seems to need it...

Whoever pulls the sword from this stone is the rightful King.

But Arthur hadn't noticed the words on the side of the stone.

Who is that with you, Merlin?

This lady has come to give you a magic sword!

Once Arthur had proved himself to be king, Merlin introduced him to the Lady of the Lake.

Arthur became king at the age of just 16. He quickly gathered brave knights around him to help defend his country and do battle with the Saxons.

During these struggles, Arthur's sword broke. The wizard Merlin told him his old sword was not important and arranged for him to meet the Lady of the Lake. She gave him a brand new sword in a jeweled scabbard. The sword's name was Excalibur, and no one could stand against its stroke, so long as it was only drawn to defend what was right.

KNIGHT FEVER!
When Britain was finally at peace, Arthur married the

The lady took Arthur to a mysterious lake...

Wha... what's that?

That is your sword, Excalibur. You must always use it to defend what is right!

HUR
ROUND TABLE

beautiful Guinevere and set up his court at Camelot. He gathered a group of knights around him, brave Sir Lancelot being the most famous.

Arthur's knights agreed to fight for what was right and good and to abide by the rules of chivalry. This word comes from the old French word *chevalerie*, meaning horse soldiery. But it came to mean behavior or a set of rules that knights were expected to follow: honesty, courtesy, and readiness to defend the weak.

THE ROUND TABLE

The center of Arthur's court was the Round Table. It was made that shape so that all who sat around it would be equal, with no one at the head or at the foot. There were seats for 150 knights, but one seat, the Siege Perilous, was left empty for many years. It could only be occupied by a pure knight who would complete the quest for the Holy Grail. This was the cup which Jesus drank from at the Last Supper and which Joseph of Arimathea used to catch drops of Jesus' blood at the Crucifixion.

King Arthur's knights spent their time practicing their skills in tournaments or going on a series of quests. They fought giants and enchanted knights,

battled against evil and magic, avenged wrongs, and saved damsels in distress. The search for the Holy Grail was their most difficult quest. After many adventures, Sir Galahad, the son of Sir Lancelot, found the Grail with his companions Bors and Percival.

When Arthur had been king for many years, his nephew (or son, according to some stories) Mordred began a revolt against him. Finally Arthur killed Mordred but was fatally wounded himself. The dying king was carried to the edge of a lake, where a mysterious boat appeared to take him to the mythical Isle of Avalon.

The bones of Arthur and Guinevere are said to be buried at Glastonbury, England. A Latin inscription on the tombstone reads "*Hic jacet Arturus, rex quondam, rexque futurus*," which means "Here lies Arthur, once the king, and the future king." It is said that when Britain is in danger, Arthur will return once more to defend it. And so the legend continues…

THE MAGIC OF MERLIN

During the Middle Ages, many people believed that magic or supernatural powers caused things to happen. Today science explains so much that few people still believe in magic.

King Arthur's most important adviser was a wizard called Merlin. His magic could tell Arthur

what would happen in the future. Only Merlin knew that Arthur was really the son of the former King of Britain, Uther Pendragon.

But Merlin's power of prophecy didn't help him when he fell in love with a wicked nymph called Nimue. She learned all his magic and then used it to trap him beneath a rock forever.

ARE THE STORIES TRUE?

★ The legendary King Arthur is probably based on a Welsh leader who lived in the fifth or sixth century. The real Arthur's reign probably started and ended in civil war, just like in the legend. But he would have worn stout leather clothing and possibly a metal helmet, and he would have fought on foot with a short sword. Real knights wearing armor and riding horses weren't around until the 12th century.

There are places all over Britain named after King Arthur. But despite traditions claiming connections with Arthur, most of them probably have nothing to do with him. For example, three of the Scilly Isles are called Great Arthur, Middle Arthur, and Little Arthur after the legendary king. The ruins of Tintagel Castle in Cornwall (shown left) now stand on the site that was supposed to have been Arthur's birthplace.

Prince of THIEVES!

Who was the mysterious man in green – the real Robin Hood?

In 1991, movie fans everywhere went crazy over a Hollywood hero. That year, not one but two mega movies were released telling the story of Robin Hood.

Hood was an English outlaw who stole from the rich to give to the poor. An ace archer, Robin hid out in the trees and caves of Sherwood Forest. From here he led his band of Merry Men in the fight against bad Prince John, in the name of good King Richard the Lionheart. Or so the Hollywood legend said. But who was the real Robin Hood – and what was he like?

THE REAL-LIFE ROBIN

Tales of this legendary outlaw have survived down the centuries through ballads and stories. These told of a champion of the poor who fought a cruel and corrupt official, the Sheriff of Nottingham. Hood became a popular folk hero and a symbol of "right against might!"

The earliest mention of this legendary hero was in 1377. Then in 1405, a writer complained about men who would rather hear tales of Robin than go to church!

Soon there were many different versions of the story in print. But tracking down the real Robin is very difficult, because thieves often copied the hero's names. In 1417, a gang of outlaws included one Frere (or Friar) Tuck, and there were Robin Hoods all over the place!

ROBERT OF LOXLEY?

The real Robin Hood could have been Robert Fitzooth, born near Loxley, Yorkshire, in about 1160. Or he could have been Robert Godberd, a rebel who became an outlaw in Sherwood Forest a hundred years later. There was even a Robin Hood who fled from the law in Yorkshire in 1225.

The trouble is, no one knows for sure. Robin (or Robert) Hood was a very common name in medieval England. The legend probably grew up as a mixture of all these real-life stories, as they were passed from person to person. In fact, some scholars believe that Robin Hood is simply a fictitious character who never really existed. ▶

MEET THE MERRY MEN

◀ **Friar Tuck** was a jolly, genial churchman with a huge appetite. He surprised many a Norman enemy with the excellence of his sword fighting.

▲ **Little John** was Robin's right-hand man, a fearless fighter of immense strength and skill. His real name was John Little but Robin nicknamed him Little John as a joke because he was so tall. He joined the band of outlaws after knocking Robin into the river in a staff fight. He was second only to Robin as an archer and even better than Robin with a staff!

Alan ▶ a'Dale was the musician of the Merry Men. He entertained them around the campfire with his singing and harp playing.

Legend has it that **Will ▶ Scarlet** was so called because of his red stockings. But historians suggest that the real Will might have been given the nickname Scarlet because he was such a bloodthirsty fighter!

Hollywood has ◀ **Maid Marian** and Robin married by Friar Tuck in Sherwood Forest. The Robin Hood legends say that she was almost as good a fighter as Robin. But the character of Marian does not appear in any Robin stories until the late 15th century.

BOX OFFICE PRINCE

★ *Hollywood has made big business out of England's outlandish outlaw. But Kevin Costner (Robin Hood: Prince of Thieves) and Patrick Bergin (Robin Hood) are just the latest in a long line of Hollywood stars who have worn the Lincoln green outfit to take on the role of Robin.*

Way back in 1922, Douglas Fairbanks, Sr., played Robin in Robin Hood, a silent version of the legend. Errol Flynn was the star in the 1938 version, The Adventures of Robin Hood. This action-packed adventure featured a sword fight between Flynn as Robin and Basil Rathbone as Sir Guy of Gisbourne and an archery contest staged by a real-life archery champion named Howard Hill.

HOLLYWOOD HEROES

Other films followed. One starred Sean Connery and Audrey Hepburn; another was a 1973 cartoon version by Disney, with animals in the starring roles.

The green good-guy has also been the subject of several

▲ *Swashbuckling heroes Errol Flynn (Robin) and Basil Rathbone (Guy of Gisbourne)*

TV series include The Adventures of Robin Hood, first broadcast in 1955, and Robin of Sherwood in 1984. Mel Brooks' 1993 movie Robin Hood: Men in Tights found some humor in Sherwood Forest.

LORD OF THE APES

The son of Lord Greystoke, Tarzan was abandoned as a baby in the African jungle and raised by apes. They adopted him as one of their own and taught him the secrets of the animals.

▲ *Branching out – Olympic swimmer Weissmuller became king of the jungle*

Tarzan battled it out against the most ferocious crocodiles, lions, and snakes. Not to mention many human enemies, including evil ivory-hunters, greedy diamond-smugglers, and cruel circus-owners who wanted to take him back to civilization.

CREEPER CRAWLER!
There have been scores of Tarzan films and many different actors have starred in the role. The best remembered is probably Johnny Weissmuller (above) who first played Tarzan in 1932. Before acting, Weissmuller was a swimmer and had competed in the Olympic Games.

AH-AAAAH-AAH! Jungle hero Tarzan was the creation of the American author Edgar Rice Burroughs. The first Tarzan book, *Tarzan of the Apes*, was published back in 1914. In all he wrote 26 Tarzan adventures and became a millionaire.

13

ANIMAL FAMILIES

Tarzan wasn't the only human raised by animals. There are lots of other stories – and some of them are true!

Romulus and Remus, the legendary founders of the ancient city of Rome, were said to have been thrown into the River Tiber when they were still babies. The story goes that they were washed ashore and rescued by a family of wolves who looked after them and treated them like their own cubs.

▲ *Company of wolves – Romulus and Remus*

THE MAN-CUB

In *The Jungle Book* by Rudyard Kipling, Mowgli was adopted by wolves and then lived with all the animals in the jungle. According to the story, Mowgli means "frog" in wolf language!

MONKEYING AROUND

In 1973 a boy was found living with a family of monkeys in Sri Lanka. He could not stand upright, but was a very nimble climber.

WOLF SISTERS

Two Indian children, Amala and Kamala, were discovered in 1920 living with a family of wolves. They ran around on all four legs, and used their highly developed sense of smell to find food. The strange story had a sad end when Amala died within a year of being rescued. Kamala survived for nine years and even learned to walk upright and speak before she died.

DEER BOY

A boy aged about 10 was discovered in 1967 living with a herd of gazelles. His ankles were thick and strong – perfect for gazelle speed and great bounding leaps. He even seemed to be able to communicate with the rest of the herd and twitched his ears just like them.

Wild child – the gazelle ▶ *boy was found in the Sahara desert*

▲ *The Greystoke legend (above) comes true! A boy in Sri Lanka was actually reared by monkeys*

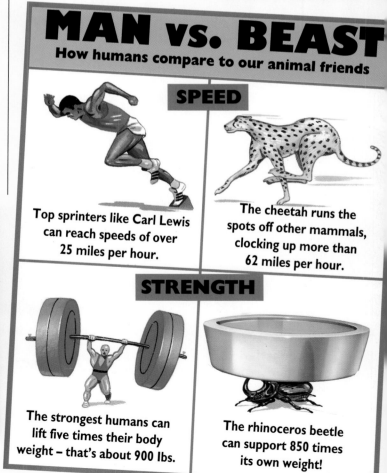

MAN vs. BEAST
How humans compare to our animal friends

SPEED

Top sprinters like Carl Lewis can reach speeds of over 25 miles per hour.

The cheetah runs the spots off other mammals, clocking up more than 62 miles per hour.

STRENGTH

The strongest humans can lift five times their body weight – that's about 900 lbs.

The rhinoceros beetle can support 850 times its own weight!

14

ALL FOR ONE

and one for all!

The original tale of *The Three Musketeers* was written by Alexandre Dumas and published in 1844.

This was the motto of the Musketeers, the king's elite bodyguard in 17th-century France. They were the best and bravest soldiers in the country – a band of swash-buckling swordsmen who had sworn to protect King Louis XIII.

In the story D'Artagnan, a young daredevil with a taste for adventure, heads off to Paris to join the king's bodyguard. No sooner does he arrive than he finds himself challenging the three Musketeers to a duel. But Athos, Porthos, and Aramis are destined to become his greatest friends and staunchest allies. Intrigue and danger stalk the four heroes' every move in their battle to defend the king.

THAT'S RICH

Cardinal Richelieu, the treacherous villain of the story, was a real person. Richelieu was ruthless and was hated throughout France by nobles and peasants alike.

But he was no traitor – in fact he served King Louis XIII faithfully for over 20 years and helped to make France one of the strongest military powers in Europe.

ARAMIS

Aramis was the studious Musketeer. His character was probably based on Henri d'Aramitz, a squire from the province of Bearn in the south of France who joined the king's Musketeers in 1640.

ATHOS

Athos hid a romantic soul beneath his casual exterior. The real Athos was Armand de Sillègue from Athos in southern France. He was a Musketeer until 1643 when he was killed fighting a duel.

PORTHOS

Porthos was tubby and jovial. He loved nothing better than playing tricks on the other Musketeers. He is based on a man called Isaac de Portau, who was born in Pau, France, and became a Musketeer in 1643.

D'ARTAGNAN

D'Artagnan was young and adventurous and went to Paris to try to join the Musketeers. The real D'Artagnan was Charles de Batz-Castlemore, a land-owner from D'Artagnan in southern France. He became a capitaine lieutenant in the king's Musketeers in 1667 and was killed at the Siege of Maastricht in 1673.

▲ Robert Redford and Paul Newman star as Butch Cassidy and the Sundance Kid

Most of the action-packed stories about gun-slinging cowboys in America's Wild West are just that – stories!

In many of these movies and books Native Americans were called "red Indians" and portrayed as murdering barbarians. But this was far from the truth. In fact thousands of Native Americans were killed by the U.S. Army as they struggled to protect their lands and their way of life.

◀Won the battle – lost the war! Sitting Bull defeated General Custer but was forced to surrender five years later

NO SURRENDER

As the population of the United States grew and spread across America, the native people were forced to give up their lands. But they weren't going to surrender without a struggle.

There were many different tribes of American Indians scattered over the plains. To defeat the might of the U.S. Army, however, they needed to unite and fight together. Leaders of the Sioux joined some of the other tribes in the struggle to protect their lands, but the fierce battles which

followed were in vain.

Today the Native Americans have lost most of their land. Many of the heroic skills they used to survive have been forgotten. Lots of movies have been made about the Wild West but some real-life heroes and villains emerged, too – American Indian chiefs, cowboys, rustlers, robbers, and lawmen – and their legend lives on.

SITTING BULL

Sitting Bull was one of the bravest and most famous of the Sioux chiefs. He led his people in a 20-year battle against the U.S. army and defeated General George Custer at the Battle of Little Bighorn in 1876. But by 1881 he had only 186 followers left and was forced to surrender. His people were promised a peaceful life on a reservation but the promises were broken and Sitting Bull was imprisoned. He was killed in 1890.

CRAZY HERO

Crazy Horse was another Sioux war chief who refused to leave the plains to the white settlers. "One does not sell the earth upon which the people walk,"

OUT WEST

When Hollywood invented the Western with its sharp-shooting stories of "cowboys and Indians" it rewrote history in the bargain.

▲ **Not for sale! Crazy Horse refused all offers for the Indians' land**

◄ **Buffalo soldier – William Cody's Wild West Show toured Europe**

he replied when offered money for the sacred Black Hills.

BUFFALO BILL

Buffalo Bill's real name was William Frederick Cody. In the early 1880s, he organized a traveling Wild West show which toured the States and Europe for over 20 years. His performers acted out the spectacular life of the West, reliving the legendary stories of cowboys, American Indians, gunfighters, soldiers, and scouts to audiences all over the world.

WYATT EARP

There have been many movies based on this legendary lawman of the West, famous for his gunfight at the O.K. Corral. But Earp was also a gambler and fighter who probably broke as many laws as he upheld.

BUTCH CASSIDY AND THE SUNDANCE KID

The real names of these two bank and train robbers were Robert Leroy Parker and Harry Longabaugh. Between 1896 and 1901, they led a band of villains called the Wild Bunch or the Hole-in-the-Wall Gang. The lawmen of the West were always hot on their trail but never managed to catch them.

In 1901 Butch and Sundance fled to South America. Legend has it that they were gunned down by soldiers in Bolivia in 1909. But for years afterward many people claimed to have seen the pair alive and well. Did Butch and Sundance stage their own disappearance and live the rest of their lives in peace? We may never know!

COWGIRLS

Annie Oakley (shown right), trick-shot star of Buffalo Bill's Wild West Show, was not really a cowgirl. Her real name was Phoebe Moses and she only ever visited the West with the show!

Daring Calamity Jane (Martha Cannary) dressed like a cowboy and packed a pistol at a time when most women were wearing long dresses and corsets!

THE LAST CRUSADER

Indiana Jones, the awesome archaeologist with a taste for adventure!

This plucky professor with his trademark leather jacket, fedora hat, and lethal bull whip is the legendary hero of three block-busting movies. An expert archaeologist, Indy's searches take him all over the world.

Wherever Indy goes, from the Andes to Egypt, danger and excitement are never far away. He battles it out with all manner of baddies, from Arabian swordsmen to Nazi soldiers. Not to mention spectacular traps designed to protect the treasure and send unwanted visitors to a grisly end.

Raiders of the Lost Ark introduces the fearless Mr. Jones on a quest to find the lost Ark of the Covenant. According to the Old Testament, this was the chest in which the Ten Commandments were sealed. Indy is after another biblical treasure, the Holy Grail, in movie number three, Indiana Jones and the Last Crusade.

Both these sacred objects have been sought by other legendary heroes (see pages 8-9). But there have been Indiana Jones-style heroes in real life as well. The most famous is probably the English treasure-hunting archaeologist Howard Carter (1873-1939).

Carter made the most sensational find of the century when, in 1922, he discovered the tomb of the pharaoh Tutankhamen in Egypt. Unlike tombs of other pharaohs, it had not been plundered by thieves and contained riches the likes of which had never been seen before.

But there was a darker side to Carter's discovery.

Three other archaeologists all died under mysterious circumstances shortly after entering the tomb. This led to stories of the Curse of the Pharaoh and claims that the treasure was protected by deadly bacteria. And you thought all archaeologists did was dig holes in the ground!

S-S-S-SCARY!
Almost all heroes have one weak spot and for Indy it's snakes. He'll happily dodge poisoned darts and wander through a pit of deadly spiders but at the first sign of a slithering serpent his knees turn to jelly!

007, LICENSED

Scottish actor Sean Connery played 007 in the very first Bond film, Dr. No, in 1962, and then in six others. He was the first actor to say the immortal words, "My name is Bond, James Bond."

O KILL!

The name's Bond, James Bond. This super-spy is more than a match for some of the movies' archvillains

▼ George Lazenby played Bond in On Her Majesty's Secret Service. *In the film his wife Teresa, Contessa di Vicenzo, (Diana Rigg), is murdered by Bond's archenemy, Blofeld.*

James Bond, 007, licensed to kill. He's the world's top secret agent. He has the special 00 code number – the number that means he is one of the British Secret Service's elite agents who are licensed to kill in the line of duty. His boss, known only by his mysterious code name, M, sends him all over the world to do battle with the enemies of his queen and country.

James Bond is hugely popular around the world. As well as the original 13 books, there have been 19 films, including a spoof version of *Casino Royale* with David Niven as James Bond and Woody Allen as his villainous nephew.

By 1989 an incredible 1.75 billion people had been to see a Bond film at the movies. Including TV showings and video rentals, about half of the world's population have seen a James Bond action movie.

TRICKS OF THE TRADE

Ian Fleming was the author of the original James Bond books. The first, *Casino Royale*, was published in 1953. Fleming went on to write 12 more Bond books.

Fleming himself had worked for British Naval Intelligence during World War II and the books featured many tricks of the trade that he had picked up.

Bond was named after an ornithologist who lived near Fleming in Jamaica. His action-packed adventures were based on those of a British spy, Sidney Reilly, and a notorious double agent, Dusko Popov.

The fifth Bond was Timothy Dalton, who played him in License to Kill. *Pierce Brosnan is the sixth Bond.*

▲Roger Moore played Bond from 1973 to 1986. He was in seven movies, using wit and charm to make them some of the best Bond films ever.

Just for laughs – David Niven as bond in the spoof 007 movie

BOND BADDIES

▼ **Jaws** was over seven feet tall, a villain with a murderous smile. He had vicious metal teeth and immense strength. Bond tried to electrocute him and throw him out of a train window, and used a magnet to pick him up by his teeth and drop him into a tank full of sharks.

◀ Bond's most hated enemy was probably **Ernst Stavro Blofeld**. He was head of SPECTRE (Special Executive for Counter Intelligence, Terrorism, Revenge and Extortion) and was the mastermind behind several attempts at world domination.

★ The Man with the Golden Gun, **Francisco Scaramanga**, was a deadly assassin. He charged $1 million for each job and used a cleverly disguised gun which he assembled from objects such as a cigarette lighter, a pen, and a cuff link. However, even this was no match for Bond's sharp shooting.

Goldfinger's manservant and bodyguard was the deadly **Oddjob**, a martial arts expert. He attacked Bond with a steel-rimmed bowler hat which he flung like a deadly frisbee.

◀ **Rosa Klebb** was a highly dangerous Soviet agent who tried to kill Bond with poisoned flick knives that shot out from the front of her shoes.

★ **Auric Goldfinger** was a villain with a taste for gold. He smuggled gold bars in the frame of his Rolls-Royce and then tried to break into the U.S. gold reserves at Fort Knox.

GADGET CRAZY

★ *To help him on his missions Bond was armed with the very latest spy gadgets cunningly disguised as everyday things. These were built for him by a top secret inventor known only as Q.*

Ian Fleming based the character of Q on a real-life gadget expert he had met during the war. Charles Fraser-Smith worked for the British government, creating devices for spies. He designed pens with maps hidden in them and hairbrushes with secret compartments. His special golf balls had compasses inside but you could still play golf with them! Fleming used this idea in Diamonds Are Forever – the diamonds were hidden inside golf balls.

▶ *This golden ring, made for KGB spies of the former Soviet Union, contains a secret camera. Now that's what you call a snappy idea!*

POW!

BATMAN
v
SUPERMAN

Who's the most powerful superhero? Is it Superman, the Man of Steel, with his incredible strength and speed? Or Batman, the Caped Crusader, the crime fighter with the armored suit and the amazing Batmobile?

Turn the page to check our superhero fact-files and decide for yourself

POWER TEST
How those super heroes measure up

Superman is from the planet Krypton. He came to Earth as a baby in a spaceship, just before his planet was destroyed by a huge explosion. His foster parents on earth were Jonathan and Martha Kent, who named him Clark. Whenever his superpowers are needed, Clark races to the nearest phone booth and emerges as Superman – ready to fly into battle with criminals everywhere.

Batman is really millionaire Bruce Wayne. When he was a boy, Bruce saw a mugger kill his parents – and from then on, he swore to devote his life to fighting crime. His Batman disguise strikes terror into the hearts of cowardly criminals. Whenever Gotham City is overrun by crime, Police Commissioner Gordon calls up Batman by shining a giant bat-signal high into the night sky.

SUPERMAN

Secret identity:	Mild-mannered reporter Clark Kent
Nicknames:	Man of Steel, Man of Tomorrow
Uniform:	Blue tights and shirt, has a yellow logo with a red S in the middle of it; red trunks, cape, and long boots
Superpowers:	X-ray vision, ability to fly, incredible strength, faster than a speeding bullet
Lives:	Metropolis
Enemy no 1:	Lex Luthor, super-criminal supreme
Other enemies:	Terra-Man, Brainiac, Mr. Mxyzptlk, Nuclear Man, and Spider Lady
Partners:	Supergirl, Lois Lane

▲ *What a super star! Christopher Reeve as Superman*

INDESTRUCTIBLE
Superman can only be killed by a green stone called Kryptonite the fragment remains of the planet Krypton.

ACTORS WHO HAVE PLAYED SUPERMAN:

Kirk Alyn
George Reeves
Christopher Reeve
John Haymes Newton
(as Superboy)
Dean Cain

HERO HISTORY

★ Superman was invented by two American teenagers, Jerry Siegel and Joe Schuster. They lived in Cleveland, Ohio, and first came up with the idea back in 1933. But it wasn't until June 1938 that the Man of Steel made his first appearance in *Action Comics No. 1*. The superhero was on the radio within three years, on film by 1948, and in the first *Superman* TV series by 1953. In 1966 there was even a *Superman* stage musical!

The best was still to come though. In 1978 *Superman* was made into a major Hollywood movie starring Christopher Reeve. And in the latest TV series, Superman is played by Dean Cain (left).

MORE COMIC SUPERHEROES

★ **Wonder Woman**
Diana Prince first appeared in a comic in 1941. Wonder Woman wears a red, white, and blue bathing suit, complete with bullet-deflecting bracelets. How chic!

★ Skinny schoolboy Peter Parker was bitten by a radioactive spider and soon developed incredible superpowers. As **Spider-Man**, he spins webs strong enough to climb up skyscrapers and ensnare his villainous enemies.

★ **Captain Marvel** was born when paperboy Billy Batson uttered the magic word "Shazam" and gained
● the wisdom of **S**olomon
● the strength of **H**ercules
● the stamina of **A**tlas
● the power of **Z**eus
● the courage of **A**chilles
● and the speed of **M**ercury.

BATMAN

Secret identity:	Millionaire playboy Bruce Wayne
Nicknames:	The Caped Crusader, The Masked Manhunter
Uniform:	Dark gray cape with blue mask and hood, black and yellow bat logo on chest. In the most recent films, Batman has favored a sinister black mask.
Superpowers:	Equipment belt with grappling hooks to scale buildings, nerve gas, and freezing compound
Lives:	Gotham City
Enemy no I:	The Joker
Other enemies:	The Penguin, The Riddler, Catwoman, Two-Face
Partners:	Robin the Boy Wonder, Alfred the butler

◀ *Batman, the Caped Crusader against crime*

HERO HISTORY

★ Batman was created by artist Bob Kane and writer Bill Finger in 1939. His first appearance was in *Detective Comics No.27* in May 1939 and he soon came up against an awesome array of fearful foes including The Penguin, who is armed with a deadly umbrella and wears a tuxedo; the Riddler with his ridiculous rhymes; and the Joker, with his grotesque green hair, who "smiles a smile of death."

The first *Batman* series was made for the movie in 1943, and in 1966 the Caped Crusader zapped onto TV starring Adam West as Batman and Burt Ward as Robin. Then came the bat-abulous movie of 1989, in which Batman was played by Michael Keaton, with Jack Nicholson as the sinister Joker. In the sequel, *Batman Returns*, the pint-sized Penguin is played by Danny DeVito.

Copies of *Detective Comics No.27* are now worth a fortune. On December 18, 1991, one sold for a whopping $50,000! Copies of this and *Action Comics No.1*, in which Superman made his first appearance, are now the most valuable in the world.

AWESOME!

These ninja nice-guys were dreamed up in the early 1980s by two comic-buffs called Kevin Eastman and Peter Laird. Working on their idea late one night, the two illustrators pulled a book on the history of art off the shelf. Eastman and Laird named the turtles after four famous Italian artists – only they made a spelling mistake, adding an extra 'a' to Michelangelo!

Each of the fab four heroes was given his own personality: Leonardo, the leader, takes responsibility for the rest of the guys; Michaelangelo is a practical joker; Raphael can get very moody; and Donatello is a genius gadget-freak!

SHELL SHOCK!

The turtles began life as ordinary pets. But after coming into contact with a puddle of radioactive slime, they mutated to become big, beefy, and superpowerful! Living in New York's sewers with their ninja master (a rat called Splinter) they spent their days pigging out on pizza and fighting the criminal ways of their archenemy, Shredder.

The first turtle comic book was published by Kevin and Peter with their own money, back in 1984. Printed in black and white, it went largely unnoticed. Luckily, licensing expert Mark Freedman spotted the fab four. Mark made it his mission to turn the turtles into superstars! But it wasn't all smooth sailing. "Everyone gave us reasons why it wouldn't work," he explains, "such as 'Green is an ugly color' or 'Whoever heard of turtles selling?' "

TURTLE POWER

Playmates Toys took on the Turtles, aiming them at children rather than teenagers and toning down the violence. Now even the baddies live on to fight another day. The action toys they produced sold in their millions.

With the turtles having their own TV cartoon show, Turtlemania really took off. Our heroes started appearing all over the place – on posters, pajamas, pencil cases, and even pizza packaging. Cries of "Cowabunga!" could be heard in classrooms all over the world.

The first blockbusting Turtle feature film made $25 million the weekend it opened in the U.S. And two more Turtle movies have ensured the fab four a place in history. As legends go, these mean, green guys are larger than life!

THE INCREDIBLE HULK! ▶

As bizarre as it may seem, being green and the product of a radioactivity accident is nothing new. Back in 1962, The Incredible Hulk made his first appearance in The Hulk comic. In 1977, he was the star of a TV series in which David Banner is exposed to gamma radiation and turns into the amazingly powerful Hulk whenever he gets angry. Totally awesome!

Today's superheroes are mighty techno icons who tackle crime with breathtaking bionic powers.

In films like *The Terminator* and *Robocop*, the heroes are cyborgs – robots that look exactly like humans. They have superhuman strength and are virtually indestructible. And as if that wasn't enough, they're also quite handy with a wrench and can repair or rebuild their own "bodies" whenever they get damaged or "injured."

BIONIC BEGINNINGS

"We have the technology, we can rebuild him!"

It all started back in 1973 when *The Six Million Dollar Man* TV movie hit the small screen. The film introduced us to Steve Austin, a chisel-jawed test pilot played by Lee Majors (above right). Austin had been badly burned in an airplane crash, but luckily, a top secret team of government doctors were able to rebuild his shattered body with bionic parts.

His legs and one arm became mechanical and he was given an extra-powerful bionic eye with telescopic vision. These gave him the speed to outrun a

INDES

▲ *Man of metal: under the skin, the sinister cyborg is none other than Arnie!*

▲ *In 1976 Steve Austin (left) teamed up with the bionic woman (above)*

Ferrari, the strength of Goliath, and the eyesight of an eagle.

In 1976 he was joined by a crime-fighting partner, Jaime Sommers, played by Lindsay Wagner. After a skydiving accident, Jaime is also rebuilt with bionic parts. Together they take on such ruthless villains as a bionic abominable snowman and a female super-crook who commands a team of highly trained sharks. Snappy stuff!

MURPHY'S LAW

In the three *Robocop* films, Peter Weller plays Murphy, a policeman who is gunned down by evil criminals in Detroit, Michigan. He is revived and rebuilt as a half-man, half-machine, mechanical police officer – Robocop.

Dressed as a modern-day knight, he wears bullet-proof armor and a helmet with a visor over his eyes. But he's not the only arresting movie star. Cop a load of Robocop's fight with a completely robotic cop, ED-209 and discover who has the strongest arm of the law!

HE'LL BE BACK!

Perhaps the most dramatic techno hero appeared in the form of the Terminator. Arnold Schwarzenegger starred in *The Terminator* and *Terminator 2: Judgment Day,* playing a powerful cyborg with incredible strength, speed, and the chilling catchphrase "I'll be back!"

In *Terminator 2* he takes on another robotic cyborg, the T1000, made of an advanced liquid metal which it uses to change into any person or object it wants to.

Up-to-the-minute special effects are used to create the amazing technical powers of top techno heroes. The budget for *Terminator 2* was a massive $100 million! But it was worth it – the film was a great success and won four scorching Oscars.

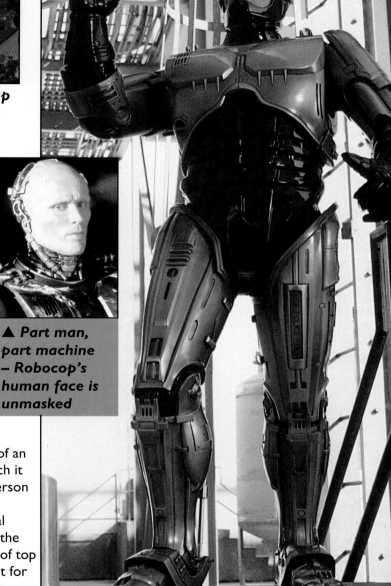

▲ *Part man, part machine – Robocop's human face is unmasked*

▲ *So who's the stiff? It's mechanical police officer Murphy!*

TRUCTIBLE!

To explore strange new worlds, to seek out new civilizations, to boldly go where no one has gone before.

This is the mission of the U.S. Starship *Enterprise* and the heroes of *Star Trek*. But Captain James T. Kirk, science officer Spock, and their daring crew are not alone as they search for adventure in outer space. The chance to discover new planets and do battle with all manner of monster aliens has provided the perfect ingredients for plenty of good hero stories. The possibilities are as endless as space itself!

COSMIC COMICS

Space heroes appeared in comic books long before they blasted off into films and television. Flash Gordon began life in a comic strip back in the 1930s. His battles with evil archenemy Ming the Merciless first appeared on screen in 1936. Then, during the 1950s and '60s, space pilot Dan Dare from the comic *Eagle* was the brightest star in the galaxy.

STARS OF STAR WARS

When it comes to intergalactic adventures the *Star Wars* films are really out of this world. Han Solo, Luke Skywalker, and Princess Leia take on the forces of Darth Vader in a desperate duel of good versus evil. And as well as the human heroes there's Chewbacca, a huge, hairy apelike creature, and radical robots C3PO and R2-D2.

So far the three block-

▲ **To the rescue in a flash – Flash Gordon!**

buster *Star Wars* movies have won 10 Oscars between them – and there are more movies on the way. May the Force be with them!

REAL SPACE STARS
● In 1961, Soviet cosmonaut Yuri Gagarin became the first man to travel in outer space.
● Valentina Tereshkova, also from the former USSR, blasted off in 1963 to become the first woman in space.
● American Neil Armstrong took one small step for a man and a giant leap for mankind when, in 1969, he was the first human to walk on the moon.

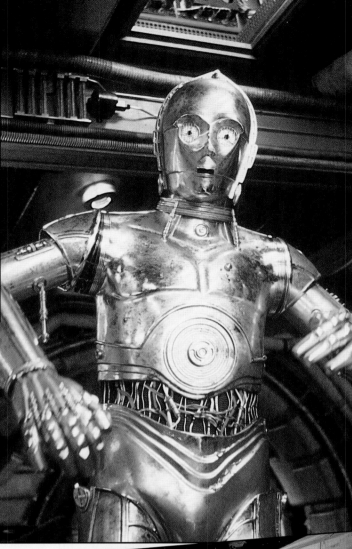

▲ **Out of this world – Star Wars' C3PO (above) and Star Trek's Starship Enterprise (right)**

SPACE
THE FINAL FRONTIER

GAME ON

A plumber and a hedgehog may be unlikely heroes – but anything can happen in computer games!

Computer games have exploded into our lives and brought us a new generation of heroes.

But the real star of these amazing adventures is the player, not the characters. Take the controls and you can become anything from a fighter pilot to an ancient warlord. It's thumb-bashing joystick action all the way in a test of lightning reactions and cunning brainpower!

Now meet two of the biggest stars in the business – Sonic and Super Mario.

MARIO MANIA

★ Mario first shot to stardom in the early 1980s in a game called *Donkey Kong*. Since then the portly plumber has been on 10 epic adventures, not to mention surprise appearances in another 12 games including *Golf* and *Tetris*. In all, more than 100 million games starring Mario have been sold worldwide – making him the most popular hero in the history of computer games!

MAGIC MARIO ▲

Name: Super Mario

Job: Plumber

Lives: Mushroom Kingdom

Created: 1981

Works for: Nintendo

Best friends: Luigi (Mario's thinner brother), Yoshi (a dinosaur), and Princess Toadstool

Worst enemy: Bowser, the King of the Koopas

ROBOTIC ROBOTNIK

★ Spiny superstar Sonic is locked in battle with the evil Dr. Robotnik. This fiendish inventor traps cute animals and forces them to join his merciless mechanical army. The latest addition to Dr. Robotnik's crew is Knuckles – a misguided pink anteater who thinks Sonic is up to no good and must be stopped.

◄ SUPER SONIC

Name: Sonic the Hedgehog

Lives: On the planet Mobius

Created: 1990

Works for: SEGA

Games: There have been six Sonic adventures so far

Best friend: A two-tailed fox known as Tails (although his real name is Miles)

INDEX